SIGNS

Written by Le Anne Barber
Photography by Diane Joy Schmidt

Celebration Press
An Imprint of Addison-Wesley
Educational Publishers, Inc.

I see signs on a bus,

signs on a store,

signs on a house,

signs on a door.

I see signs on boxes,

signs in a zoo,

signs on a school,
and signs on you!